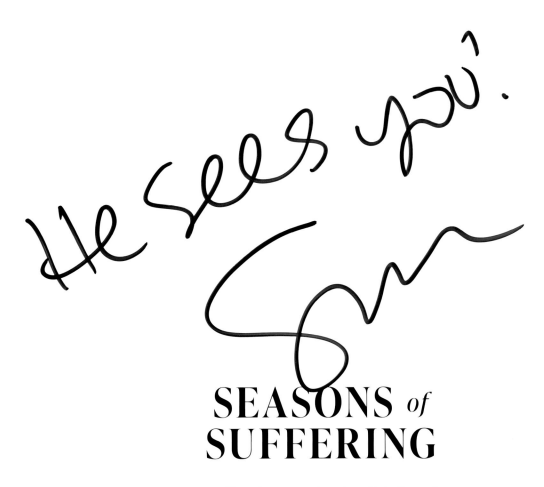

He sees you.

SEASONS *of* SUFFERING

Reflections on Doubt, Grief, and
Mental & Spiritual Healing

SHELBY TSIKA MARQUARDT

2023–Sea Harp An imprint of Nori Media Group

P.O. Box 310, Shippensburg, PA 17257-0310
"Be Much Occupied with Jesus"

Cover design and interior page design copyright 2023. All rights reserved.

This book and all other Sea Harp books are available at Christian bookstores and distributors worldwide.

For more information on foreign distributors, call 717-532-3040.

Reach us on the Internet: www.seaharp.com

ISBN 13 HC: 978-0-7684-7577-7

ISBN 13 EBook: 978-0-7684-7578-4

For Worldwide Distribution, Printed in China

2 3 4 5 6 / 26 25 24

SEASONS *of* SUFFERING

Reflections on Doubt, Grief, and
Mental & Spiritual Healing

SHELBY TSIKA MARQUARDT

SEA HARP PRESS

DEDICATION

To my husband, Cody. My partner in suffering, joy, sadness, laughter and everything in between from now until eternity. Thank you for cheering me on and being by my side in this life. You are my greatest treasure apart from Christ.

PREFACE

Seasons of Suffering is for sufferers, born out of the deepest sorrows of my life thus far. These thoughts and meditations are near to my heart. They were all written in odd places. At home on the couch when the pain was so deep I couldn't go to work, in the car outside my counselor's office, after panic attacks, and in my bed during my countless sleepless nights. My writing began as a way to cope with all my hurt and doubt.

I've known Jesus since I was little and I can't quite remember a time I didn't know Him. I do, however, remember the first time I doubted His goodness.

The summer my aunt Kim died of leukemia, I was 11 years old. We were very close, so much closer than normal aunts and nieces typically are. I remember so much of that summer. Wanting to be near her, I begged to be able to go with my mom to what would be her last hospital stay. I remember the way it felt to be barricaded behind the recliner in her hospital room with my coloring book while she threw up endlessly from the chemo treatments. I remember when we were told they were preparing her for hospice care. I remember the smell of her hospital—I can't walk into one to this day without being taken right back to that summer.

Grappling with death at 11 years old set the tone for my teens. In high school, I began to experience clinical anxiety and depression. I did not have the words for what I was experiencing at the time, and I could not understand why the feelings of intense dread and anxiety plagued me. Unfortunately, for years I would go on to mistake these feelings that would come and go for the voice of God. This was a deep internal wound that created scars I still have today.

I lost my grandfather to cancer when I was in high school, and carrying the weight of grief and loss again felt horribly familiar. Seeing my mom and grandmother hurt was the worst part.

After his death, my grandmother would soon begin to have a ton of health issues. Cancer and brain surgery and then more cancer. She would die the summer I got married in 2019. Again, a familiar grief. An ache for losing a third member of my family. I have the happiest childhood memories with my mother's side of the family. My family, the one that was once so close, reduced to a broken thing. Chipped away at, bit by bit until all that was left was rubble. If you have experienced loss, you know what it is to experience the shift in dynamic that hurts almost more than the loss itself. We do not only grieve the people we lose, but the piece they were in the family unit. For us, we lost the glue.

In the summer of 2018 I had my first panic attack. There is a stigma surrounding panic attacks and everyone has a different idea of what they are. You may picture me bringing a paper bag to my mouth and breathing in and out very quickly or me falling to the ground. If you have experienced one—a real one—you know how awful they can be and how severely lacking

TV depictions of them are. Mine was horrid. My brain was truly convinced I was dying. My whole body was shaking, I had chills up my spine, my heart was having palpitations, I felt intense doom and dread, my vision became blurry and I became dizzy. I honestly thought I was having a heart attack or a brain aneurysm. Later, I would genuinely ask my doctor for an EKG and a brain scan.

This attack began a two month long debilitating season of panic attacks, medication and a whole lot of surrendering to the Lord. I had reactions to my first medication. My body involuntarily shook and twitched for 24 hours. I could not eat. I lost about 30 pounds. It caused more panic attacks. I remember one day having seven in a row. I truly did not see a way out of the state I was in. I had just gotten engaged, and would look down at my ring in between panics and wonder if I would have to give it back. I did not see myself ever being able to be alone, drive, work or feel normal again.

The Lord brought me out of that season and has healed so many pieces of me. Since 2018, I have had a few flare ups of panic attack seasons. I have been on and off medications and endured all that it entails. I have learned so much and I am so grateful for my counselors, my family and friends who have walked with me through my darkest times.

This is not an exhaustive, detailed list of all the pain I have experienced throughout my life. I tell you some of the "big ones" not to give myself some sort of stamp of approval to write on suffering, but to show that I know what it is to experience grief, loss, trauma, mental health battles, and in turn, deep doubts in my faith.

I know what it is to lie awake at night and wonder if God hears you and if He even exists. To wonder if I can trust the Book I have been rooted in since I was little. I know what it's like to wrestle with and fight for your faith when the only reason you have for staying is the same reason Simon Peter had, recorded in the sixth chapter of the Gospel of John:

"From this time many of his disciples turned back and no longer followed him. "You do not want to leave too, do you?" Jesus asked the Twelve. Simon Peter answered him, "Lord, to whom shall we go? You have the words of eternal life" (John 6:67-68 NIV).

Simon Peter did not see anywhere else to go that made any sense. He chose to stay in the faith. He chose to surrender his opinions about Jesus's hard teachings and trust He was telling the truth. He rested in the mystery of Christ.

My heart in creating this book is rooted in **2 Corinthians 1:3-7:**

*Blessed be the God and Father of our Lord Jesus Christ, the Father of mercies and God of all comfort, who comforts us **in all our affliction**, so that we may be able to comfort those who are in **any** affliction, with the comfort with which we ourselves are comforted by God. For as we share abundantly in Christ's sufferings, so through Christ we share abundantly in comfort too. If we are afflicted, it is **for your comfort and salvation;** and if we are comforted, it is **for your comfort**, which you experience when you patiently endure the same sufferings that we suffer. Our hope for you is unshaken, for we know that as you share in our sufferings, **you will also share in our comfort.***

A few things I want you to notice about that passage:

1. If we suffer greatly, it makes us empathetic people. I may not be writing about the same things you have personally been through in this book, but I know what it's like to feel deep pain, loss, to not know if you'll ever be the same again or even make it through a devastating season.

2. One of the most precious ways people are comforted in their time of pain and hurting is being able to talk with someone who has experienced the same pain. This is a life-giving way to view your own suffering, and an exciting way to view the comfort and lessons you receive in the valley. For me, all I've been through, and all the Lord has taught me is (in part, at least) for your comfort. Yes, you, reader of this book!

3. We will be comforted. God comforts and teaches us in our affliction. What a good Father! Our sufferings are not wasted. Not one ounce of it is in vain. Not one dreadful day filled with perceived hopelessness is without purpose.

I pray that you find comfort in these pages written by a fellow sufferer, wrestler and doubter. I pray you surrender your own ideas of who He is and lay it all at His feet. He will pick it all up and sort it for you. In the meantime, try to rest in His abundant grace that is always there for you.

THE PHOTOGRAPHS

The photographs that accompany my writings,
Scripture, and the quotes on the pages that follow are
all photos captured on my travels and wanderings. This
book is truly an outpouring of my soul, filled with my art,
written and visual. I pray as you read each page, each image
brings you peace. I pray you can find a couple of favorites
that turn into the quiet place you go to in your head when
you need a reprieve from your day, or just a place you
picture yourself relaxing. I pray you are inspired by my
photographs and feel how it feels to be in each place.

*Some of the photographs in this book are available
for purchase in print-form on my website below.*

www.shelbytsikamarquardt.com

"As Andrew Greely said, *'If one wishes to eliminate uncertainty, tension, confusion and disorder from one's life, there is no point in getting mixed up either with Yahweh or with Jesus of Nazareth.'*

I grew up expecting that a relationship with God would bring order, certainty, and a calm rationality to life. Instead, I have discovered that living in faith involves much dynamic tension."

Philip Yancey

15

HIS PURPOSES

I'm hit out of nowhere.
The searing pain of the emotional blow
shocks me and shakes me so much that it
is physical in more ways than one. It hurts
all over.
The doom.
The despair.
The darkness.

How can a human feel
this much hurt?
Where did it come from?
Do you see me, God?

I worry I won't be provided with the
strength to get through.

That maybe, I'll always feel this way.
I remind myself that this is a lie from the
enemy of my soul.
My God goes behind
and before me.
He will fulfill His purpose for me.
He never leaves or forsakes me.

This life is a vapor,
our thoughts...a breath.

Every ounce of suffering is filled to the
brim with good purposes of the One who
holds me in His hand and never lets go.

A 3AM PRAYER

It feels like I'm missing something, sometimes.
Like Christianity is easy for everyone else.
Something is wrong with me.
I know others have struggles and even have clinical afflictions,
obsessive intrusive thought, panic attacks, depression...
I must have it the very worst, though, because it is all
attacking my faith all at once.

My faith, I will never ever leave it.
Because You, Lord, I could never leave.
The fear of losing it is very present, though.
Sometimes I stay for the sheer fear of the unknown
of this life and the next without You...
There is no other God but You, that I am sure of.
It's You or nothing.
And I don't believe there is nothing.

Sometimes I stay because I am in truly a
wonderful, peaceful state with You.
I deeply want to rest peacefully in Your loving arms.
What is holding me back right now?
The awful feelings and terrors I get sometimes that
don't match up with where my beliefs and trust lie.
I truly believe that You created this place for us to enjoy.
And oh how sweet it will be when we can enjoy it with You fully.
Oh, teach me how to rest in You.
Please, Lord.
Teach me how to better fend off my
flesh and the enemy's attempts at me.
Help me always remember who wins in the
end and that it is finished.
Give me assurance that I am safe in Your hand.

I cry aloud to God,
aloud to God, and he will hear me.
In the day of my trouble I seek the Lord;
in the night my hand is stretched out without wearying;
my **soul refuses to be comforted.**
When I remember God, I moan;
when I meditate, **my spirit faints.**
You hold my eyelids open;
I am **so troubled that I cannot speak.**
I consider the days of old,
the years long ago.
I said, "Let me remember my song in the night;
let me meditate in my heart."
Then my spirit made a diligent search:
"Will the Lord spurn forever,
and never again be favorable?
Has his steadfast love forever ceased?
Are his promises at an end for all time?
Has God forgotten to be gracious?
Has he in anger shut up his compassion?"

Psalm 77:1-9 (ESV)

"The deepest things I have learned in my own life have come from the deepest suffering. And out of the deepest waters and the hottest fires have come the deepest things I know about God."

Elisabeth Elliot

YOUR VOICE

I feel so frustrated.
So unable to see beyond the feelings that I feel.
I do not know how to hear You.
Am I supposed to, outside of Your Word?
Why do we have feelings?
I suppose they are helpful often,
but they can be so incredibly painful.

How do You speak, Lord,
when I feel so many things all at once?
Surely it's not through emotion or feeling.
The inconsistencies would be too great.
People say things like,
"I have peace about this" or
"God told me that...".

Are we sure it wasn't just your own feelings
about the issue that you are inquiring of,
manifested into feelings of peace?

How do I hear You and not mistake feeling for Your voice?
I was reminded this week that Jesus often asked
more questions of people than He answered.
Direct answers were incredibly rare.
As I meditate on this, I'm so thankful for The Word.
May I always read it and put my feelings to the test,
May I set them right when they are wrong,
May I never confuse flesh for Spirit.
Let Your voice be the loudest one I hear.

The LORD knows the
thoughts of man.
That they are
a mere breath.

Psalms 94:11 (NASB1995)

ALL THE BROKEN THINGS

Medication. I hate it, I really do.
I love the grace of it, butI really hate that I need it sometimes.
I feel weaker than those around me and petrified of side affects.
Will I be a victim of the dreaded black box warning?

Lord protect me. Lord help me through.
Remind me that You are sovereign over this.
There is no perfect solution here.
Remind me that "trusting in You alone"
does not mean that I never accept medication for help.
It really does help.

They say to try and heal the "natural" way.
But isn't nature broken, too?
Is broken nature
plus a broken human
in a broken world...
really any better than
broken medication
plus broken doctors
plus a broken me
in a broken world?

Maybe for some, and maybe sometimes for me.
But does it matter? Does it really matter what we do?
We are all just doing our best in our afflictions,
leaning on the common graces we are given.
Regardless of what we choose,
in between now and my numbered day,
not one broken thing will go to waste.
He will use all the broken things to gently teach me.
He will use them to shape me and mold me into
something with less cracks and dents
until I am something new entirely.
In all the broken things, there is a beauty
that we can't fully comprehend.

EMPTY WORDS

I reach out for guidance in my affliction,
and I am disappointed.
The church-y sentiments sting my soul.
They feel empty and useless
in this season of wrestling.

"Count it all joy"
"Take every thought captive"
"Cast your anxieties on God, He cares for you!"

How do I apply these sentiments?
What happens when I try to apply them,
and nothing changes?
I realize these sentiments are the Word of God.
They are the truest of true pieces of advice.
So, why can't I successfully apply them?
Is the point to apply them and
not always receive relief?

I think we only really know and
feel the true-ness of
some things in the Word when the
Holy Spirit teaches us those things Himself.
They are teachings deep within our souls,
born through pain and trials.
The Scriptures that feel empty in our suffering, will
hold so much weight at the proper time.

DOUBTS

I see the Church divided on so many things.
Different opinions on who is saved and who is not.
Who is worthy, if we are worthy or if we are not.
We are enough for God,
but also aren't because that's why Jesus came.
I feel like I'm bobbing in the ocean.
Sometimes overtaken by waves of
doubt, unbelief, and pain.

I bob up above the waves, only to be taken by
another wave of guilt,
shame, and intrusive thought.
Sometimes these intrusive thoughts
come out of nowhere and do not feel like my own.
They feel like my brain abandoning me
and abandoning the God I love,
but don't know for certain exists.

I know a God exists. But Jesus?
Is He really God? I think so.
How do I know?
How do I know God loves me?
How do I know I'm chosen on days I am
so filled with doubt and questioning?

Feelings are so incredibly fleeting.
I pray for peace and I often receive relief.
I want to rest in that experience, but I can't.
There has to be more certainty out there.

"We were promised
sufferings. They were part
of the program. We were even
told, 'Blessed are they that
mourn,' and I accept it. I've got
nothing that I hadn't bargained
for. Of course it is different
when the thing happens to
oneself, not to others, and in
reality, not imagination."

C.S. Lewis

COLLATERAL DAMAGE

You say You feed the birds of the air, but they, too, starve and die.
A passage of Scripture so dear to my heart plagued me with a bit of anxiety.
If I am more valuable than the birds, should I not be kept from this suffering?
Feed me, Lord. Clothe me.

I guess the truth of the matter is that You do feed me and clothe me.
You equip me with everything I need for Your good purposes.
There is a time to starve and die, yes.
And many times I will suffer in this life
and feel as though You are not providing what *I think I need.*

But You do provide.
You provide exactly what I need to fulfill Your purpose and plans for me.
For Your glory *and* my good.

That last part is what I did not believe to be true for so long.
Yes, I thought all this pain could be used for Your glory,
but my good didn't matter as much to You as Your *greater* good.
I was collateral damage.
Resentment came.
Am I just a puppet?

But that's not who You are.
You care so deeply about Your kids.
The hurtful things I go through in this life may not be anything I would have chosen,
but they are given to shape me and form me to look more like Your Son.
You take my broken pieces and shape me into something
beautiful for the benefit of all involved.
I am not collateral damage.
I am deeply seen, known, and loved.

Look at the birds of the air: they neither sow nor reap nor gather into barns, and yet your heavenly Father feeds them. Are you not of more value than they? And which of you by being anxious can add a single hour to his span of life? And why are you anxious about clothing? Consider the lilies of the field, how they grow: they neither toil nor spin, yet I tell you, even Solomon in all his glory was not arrayed like one of these. But if God so clothes the grass of the field, which today is alive and tomorrow is thrown into the oven, will he not much more clothe you, O you of little faith?

Matthew 6:26-30 (ESV)

We rejoice in our sufferings, knowing that suffering produces endurance, and endurance produces character, and character produces hope, and hope does not put us to shame, because God's love has been poured into our hearts through the Holy Spirit who has been given to us.

Romans 5:3-5 (ESV)

"He lists hope at the end, instead of where I would normally expect it, at the beginning, as the fuel that keeps a person going. No, hope emerges from the struggle, a byproduct of faithfulness."

Philip Yancey

OUT OF THIS WORLD

Sometimes I wake up and the
Gospel just feels so unreal.
Is it really our reality?
It feels too good to be true,
too weird to be true,
too confusing to be true...
So, what brings my soul back?
What makes it believe?

When I am in the depths of this feeling,
I come back to Him every time.
Some would say it's Him calling me back or reigning me in,
Some would say it's me running toward Him and
placing faith in Him of my own free will.
Maybe it's some combination that
our minds were made to not comprehend here.
I am inclined to believe the latter.
My brain hurts trying to know these mysteries.

I do not understand it all,
but I know I love Him.
The Gospel may feel
strange and out of this world,
but that's because it truly is.

How long, LORD? Will you forget me
forever? How long will you hide your
face from me?
**How long must I wrestle with my
thoughts and day after day have
sorrow in my heart?** How long will
my enemy triumph over me?

Look on me and answer, LORD my
God. Give light to my eyes,
or I will sleep in death,
and my enemy will say,
"I have overcome him," and my foes
will rejoice when I fall.
But I trust in your unfailing
love; my heart rejoices
in your salvation.
I will sing the LORD's praise,
for he has been good to me.

Psalm 13 (NIV)

RUBBLE

It's been years now.
I'm supposed to be okay with it.
Grief is like a rogue wave...
all at once, it can crash over you.
All-consuming, knocking
your feet out from under you
in a second.

Will I ever be the same?
Definitely not. How can I?
I don't see the purpose in her death.
We all die, yes, but why so early?
Why cancer? Why her?

There's rubble everywhere
from the loss of her.
Rubble and brokenness
and pain
and *lost* people.

I do not see what good there
is in her being with You.
She still had a purpose to
complete here.

Will I remember her in Heaven?
Will I get to hug her and cry
tears of joy and victory?
I know You wipe away every tear,
but happy crying is my
favorite emotion.
I hope we get to do that in Heaven.

Oh how I long to hug her
with tears streaming down my face,
feeling and knowing every
ounce of the redemption
that took place
through her story here on earth.

47

You gave us up to be devoured like sheep and have scattered us among the nations.
You sold your people for a pittance, gaining nothing from their sale.
You have made us a reproach to our neighbors, the scorn and derision of those around us.
All this came upon us, though we had not forgotten you; we had not been false to your covenant.
Our hearts had not turned back; our feet had not strayed from your path.
But you crushed us and made us a haunt for jackals; you covered us over with deep darkness.
If we had forgotten the name of our God or spread out our hands to a foreign god,
would not God have discovered it, since he knows the secrets of the heart?
Yet for your sake we face death all day long; we are considered as sheep to be slaughtered.
Awake, Lord! Why do you sleep? Rouse yourself! Do not reject us forever.
Why do you hide your face and forget our misery and oppression?
We are brought down to the dust; our bodies cling to the ground.
Rise up and help us; rescue us because of your unfailing love.

Psalm 44:11-13,17-26 (NIV)

"We feel pain as an outrage; Jesus did too, which is why he performed miracles of healing. In Gethsemane, he did not pray, 'Thank you for this opportunity to suffer,' but rather pled desperately for an escape. And yet he was willing to undergo suffering in service of a higher goal. In the end he left the hard questions ('if there be any other way . . .') to the will of the Father, and trusted that God could use even the outrage of his death for good."

Philip Yancey

EBEE'S POEM

In my journey with God I
keep waiting for a ball to drop.
Some ball, some big ball
just designed to crush me.
I have been battered by this life,
by confusion, and by the devil himself.

The longer I wait for God to be
the source of a dropped ball,
the more times His kindness is
chiseled into my experience.
Hyper-spiritual people
warn me of this ball.
They make me feel like I can't
trust my God-given instincts.
"Deep down, God is not pleased,"
they imply.

We can never be holy enough.
This is true.
That's why Jesus came,

but nothing is ever good enough for them.
Even Jesus doesn't seem
to be good enough.
What is real?
What is true anymore?

I start to question.
I feel like I'm going crazy.
It's a war between my God and theirs.
I wish I had better words to explain
what all this is like,
but for now,
for tonight,
I remember there has never
been a time in my life when
God's love for me has not
eased the blow.

No matter how big the ball,
no matter how far the drop,
my God is always there for me.

He does not hold the ball in his hand
He does not drop it on me.
He most certainly doesn't hurl it at me.

This is not what I expected.
He holds me in His hand.
I burrow into the holes He got
when He hung for me.
The ball dropped on Him then
and He withstood the weight.

It drops on me now, right into His hand.
I am remarkably unscathed.
I am deep and safe within His scars.
This is a grace-paved place.
He loves me.
This is forever.

Elizabeth (Ebee) Cochran

A sweet friend whose faith story parallels my own in so many ways.
To know her is to love her and feel seen and understood.

LOVE'S WILL

I am a vapor.
My life, a fleeting dream.
My thoughts are a breath,
my works, done and gone.

What, then, shall I do with
this time I've been given?
Does it matter?
It is of no use if it is all for me.
It matters to God, it seems.
The impact of my fleeting dream
stays with others more
than it benefits me.

I guess Jesus was right when
He told us that it is right to love
Him and others above all things.
For what is the point if we do not?
If our souls are in fact made to
be eternal and our life here...
A minuscule spec of that eternity...
We must use our spec to do the will
of the One who allowed it to
exist in the first place.

What a mercy it is for that Will to be love.
Suffering has no match when
Love Himself is working in it,
using each of our stories to help
us love Him and our neighbor more fully.

THE GIVER OF MERCIES

Each morning His mercies are new, but lately
it feels as though each morning I wake with a punch to the gut.
What is the purpose in this?
I don't see it.
The guilt comes as swiftly as the punch.
Why can't I just trust in Him?

I am learning more and more that
"trusting in Him" does not mean what I thought.
It is not a requirement to wake immediately to a feeling of
uninhibited happiness and recognition of His new mercies to be deemed a faithful
follower.

Rather, it's in resting in the truth that the mercies are there,
despite my feelings... Seeking to see them in every minute of my day.
Focusing on the Giver of the mercies and His love for me.
That is proof of my trusting in Him.

BETTER THAN ME

There is a piece of my soul that hurts
deeply when even a slight indication of
favor is given to another instead of me.

Little nothings are salt on this old wound.
A friend getting coffee with someone else,
seeing a get-together I wasn't invited to
posted online, my husband needing to
study instead of our usual evening time
together...

Bigger things feel like the wound is
split open all over again:
A horrible, painful loss of friendship,
being misunderstood completely by a
person you thought deeply knew you,
A criticism, tainted with dislike and
judgment...

I think to myself in the big and small
moments, "There's always something or
someone better than me..."

I'm working out where this
wound came from.
Maybe you have one, too?
You know the one.
The one that reminds you
how worthless you really are,

how prone you are to seeking that
missing worth from humans or yourself,
only to feel worse.

It's not that we are actually worthless.
We are not!
But simply saying,
"I am worthy"
doesn't give you worth.
Stating something does not make it true.
So, am I of value?
What makes it so?

The Creator of the universe
that gives this life meaning
gave *you* meaning.
He gave us a purpose.
Viewing ourselves and our
wounds without Christ in the equation...
is truly meaningless.
Praise God He is in this messy equation.
Praise God for making me with
worth and a purpose.
No one can take that from us.

Remembering this heals my
gaping wound from the inside.
It heals it from the root like no empty,
self-love drenched bandaid ever could.

THE MASK

Before leaving the house,
she runs to fix her mask in place.
If she left her at home,
she would be wide open,
vulnerable to attack.
Her mask that the world sees
is so much better
than she could ever be.

She is
cool,
easy,
go with the flow.

She is
effortlessly creative,
beautiful,
gentle.

She is wise beyond her years,
liked by everyone she meets.

She is a shapeshifter
throughout our day,
becoming exactly what they
would have her be.

I wonder what they would think of
the woman that hides behind her?
The one that is too easily irritated,
needs a well-thought-out
plan to be spared of stress.

The one who is chronically
self-conscious and puts in
an exuberant
amount of effort into her
creative endeavors, never feeling like
she measures up.
The weight of the invisible
standards are crushing.
She is an old soul with
impostor-syndrome,

seeking wisdom but never
knowing if she got it right.
She is much too needy,
snaps at her husband
for no reason,
battles pride,
jealousy,
the urge to lie to make
herself sound better than she is.

She is broken.
Full of sin.

The Creator knows all of this.
He knows what is behind every mask,
no matter
how cleverly placed.
He says she is seen.
He says she is loved.
Will she believe Him
enough to finally remove it?

REST

The evening is normally my favorite time
of the day. It begins with a sky painting,
created by the Creator. Warm colors and
soft, streaming light that fills my soul to the
brim.

I'm done for the day.
Rest is here and sleep is
coming soon.
Sometimes, I long for its
sweet comfort.
Sometimes, just the escape
from the battles I face.

Sleep.
The greatest gift humans
could have been given.
When it's taken from us
in the seasons we most long for it,
it feels like a cruel joke.

Every emotion, intensified.
The irritability? Off the charts.

I remind myself that He will sustain me.
No matter the hours I get,
or how bad I feel...
He provides exactly what I need.
Sleep or none.

So, I choose to focus on the hours I am
given to lie awake alone as an opportunity
to talk to Him.

To know Him more.
To seek His comfort.
To thank Him that I have
this extra time to do so.
To thank Him for the
opportunity to rest in Him
when my eyes won't stay shut.

"Mental pain is less dramatic than physical pain, but it is more common and also more hard to bear. The frequent attempt to conceal mental pain increases the burden: it is easier to say 'My tooth is aching' than to say 'My heart is broken.'"

C.S. Lewis

THE MAKER OF ME

Here I am again.
Having my own ideas about
who I'd like You to be.

A list of what I feel is
most good...
most fair...
most true for You to be,
to me.

I wrestle.
I worry.

Until I decide to lay down
my list at Your feet.
I want who You are,
not who I want You to be.

I pray, once again, for help.
For You to gather the pieces of me that don't
understand and remind them again
to trust in
the Maker of me.

Rejoice in the Lord always; again I will say, rejoice. Let your reasonableness be known to everyone. The Lord is at hand; do not be anxious about anything, but in everything by prayer and supplication with thanksgiving let your requests be made known to God. And the peace of God, which surpasses all understanding, will guard your hearts and your minds in Christ Jesus.

Finally, brothers, whatever is true, whatever is honorable, whatever is just, whatever is pure, whatever is lovely, whatever is commendable, if there is any excellence, if there is anything worthy of praise, think about these things. What you have learned and received and heard and seen in me—practice these things, and the God of peace will be with you.

Philippians 4:4-9 (ESV)

THE GOOD SHEPHERD

Was it the urgency, dread and despair? Or was it the searing doubt of You? Did the anxiety come like a creature, looking for something to latch its hands around? Or was the thought what provoked the feelings of dread? "Can I trust what You say?"

Maybe it built up. Over time, little doubts stacking one by one on top of each other. Questions I'll never know the answers to until Heaven, and maybe not even then. It feels as though my salvation is hanging in the balance. The sting is great. But then, feelings lie.

I shove it down. I don't examine it. Fear of opening the Good Book creeps in. I'm right where my enemy wants me. I pray into what feels like a void. I beat on Your chest, telling You how much I don't understand. You take it. You leave the ninety-nine to come after me. My feelings are still screaming lies to me when I begin bringing every doubt to You. I remember Your love for me, even though I still question it. We examine each doubt together. It still hurts. You place trusted saints around me. I have to talk about it this time. I'm lucky, because I'm met with so much grace.

My anxiety fades as I continue bringing myself to You each day. It's slow, but You are teaching me something. I'm a fraction stronger. I don't have answers, but I don't have to. The One I'm inquiring of is trustworthy. I humble myself and pick up my cross. His ways are better than mine. No matter how I feel. Where else shall I go?
I will continue following the Good Shepherd.

HOME

Before I knew it, I was in the wilderness.
Lost, with no idea how to get home.
The shadows grew darker with each minute
that passed by. Could I make it out?
Night came, and it was like a pit of
all-consuming blackness.
I prepare my heart to disappear from this
earth. There's no way I make it out alive.
But as soon as the night came, I felt streams
of light that shone through the leaves of the
towering trees above.
The warmth of it gives me a hope that pierces
the very depths of me.
A hope that leads me out into a place where I
can once again see where I am going.
I am still on my way home.

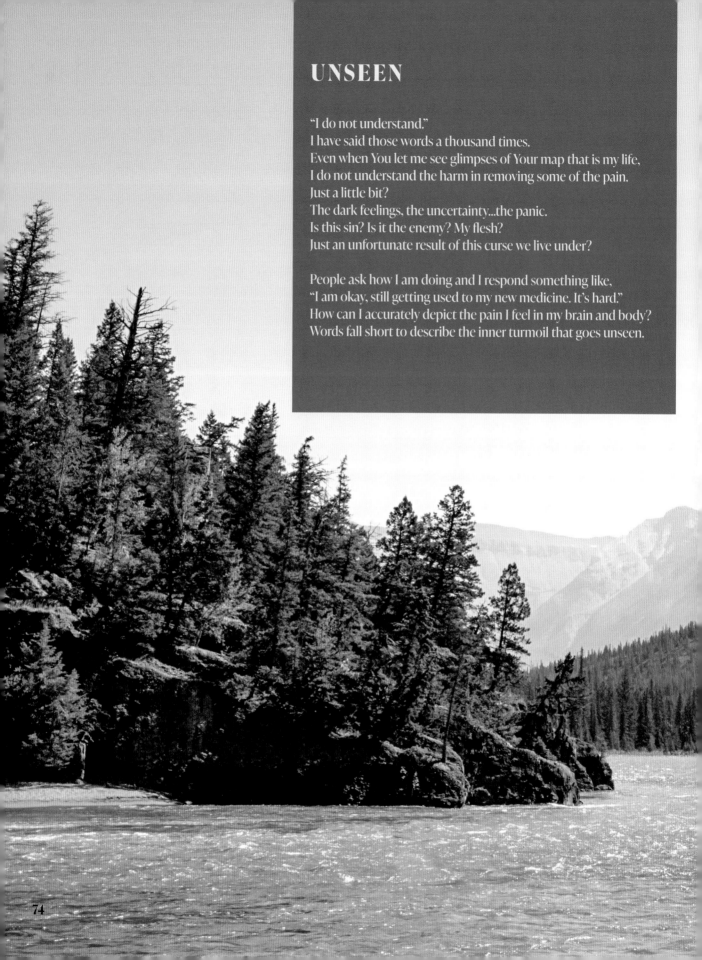

UNSEEN

"I do not understand."
I have said those words a thousand times.
Even when You let me see glimpses of Your map that is my life,
I do not understand the harm in removing some of the pain.
Just a little bit?
The dark feelings, the uncertainty...the panic.
Is this sin? Is it the enemy? My flesh?
Just an unfortunate result of this curse we live under?

People ask how I am doing and I respond something like,
"I am okay, still getting used to my new medicine. It's hard."
How can I accurately depict the pain I feel in my brain and body?
Words fall short to describe the inner turmoil that goes unseen.

"I once read the sentence 'I lay awake all night with a toothache, thinking about the toothache and about lying awake.' That's true to life. Part of every misery is, so to speak, the misery's shadow or reflection: the fact that you don't merely suffer but have to keep on thinking about the fact that you suffer. I not only live each endless day in grief, but live each day thinking about living each day in grief."

C.S. Lewis

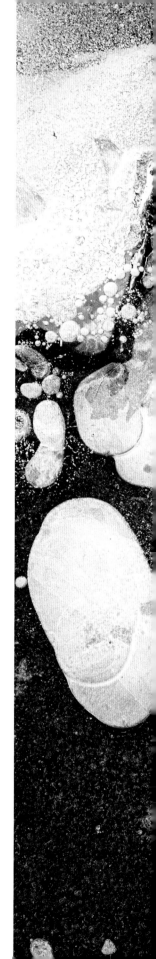

All was well with me, but he shattered me;
he seized me by the neck and crushed me.
He has made me his target;
his archers surround me.
Without pity, he pierces my kidneys and
spills my gall on the ground.
Again and again he bursts upon me;
he rushes at me like a warrior.
I have sewed sackcloth over my skin and
buried my brow in the dust.
My face is red with weeping,
dark shadows ring my eyes;
yet my hands have been free of violence
and my prayer is pure.

Job 16:12-17 (NIV)

PRAISES THROUGH TEARS

I see joy all around me.
Faith with a civilized smile.
I am supposed to respond
with sentiments that match
but it feels like a lie.
I can't match the tones.
I'm not there yet.
I feel angry.

Then, almost immediately, anxious.
Why am I angry at the joyful noise of loving God?
It's because I'm hurting.
My relationship with Him is deep and difficult right now.
I can't find the uninhibited wonder and awe that others do.
I don't have the words.
I cling to the truths I know in the depths of my soul.
He is loving.
He is just.
He is so trustworthy and good.
I don't feel the truths. I just know that they are true.
I live another day reminding myself
that my faith is not inadequate.
That He accepts my praises through tears.
That He is with me in the storm.

DARKNESS, MY FRIEND

You sting like no other.
I am hopeless and alone when you are here.
You remind me of my ever-present weakness.
You make me question all I know.
You are a strange comfort, too.
When you are upon me, this is how it should be.
I don't have to worry I am too happy.
It's what He wants. After all, in my weakness He is strong.
I don't like you, but I need you.
When you leave, something is wrong.
Come back, my suffering.
In you, I feel I am earning my place.

But what if my suffering...
This side effect of the brokenness that surrounds me...
What if God hates it all, too?
What if my pain hurts His heart?
What if He's as ready for it to end as I am?

I get frustrated and anxious sometimes when I
see people smiling in church.
I guess I am taking them
at face value, but still.
Do they not understand
the questions out there?
How are they so content?
What do they *really* believe?
Have they questioned their faith?

Jesus.
I tense up at His name when I hear it used on
the internet and by strangers now.
What will they say about Him?
Are they using Him as a cultural,
southern stamp of righteousness
or do they know Him?
Is it somewhere in between?
Is there an in between?

HELP
MY
UNBELIEF

I saw a t-shirt today that said,
"all I need is dry shampoo, coffee and Jesus"
My brain doesn't get
how we got here.
How are we using His name in this way?
If Jesus is who He says He is in His word,
how are we not more reverent?
How are we using Him in the same
list of things we need as coffee and dry
shampoo?

I hear jokes in movies about
the creation story.
The Bible, Jesus and
His resurrection...
They have influenced
our culture so heavily.
Do other people notice this, too?
Do they care?

What do I believe?
Where do I fit in this world of ideas,
or lack thereof, about Jesus?

I love Him. I've always said I loved Him.
But was it cultural at times?
Do I say it because my parents raised me to?
Was I using Him as a mascot
to feel better about myself?
Or worse, to feel superior to my peers?

I have definitely done that.
I didn't understand the magnitude of Him.
I didn't understand the weight
of Him being *God*.
My heart aches.
I'm sorry.
I believe,
help my unbelief, Lord.

"Where there is no longer
any opportunity for doubt,
there is no opportunity for
faith either."

Philip Yancey

ONE MORE ANXIOUS THOUGHT

I used to think I had to be on the lookout for You.
That I was always at risk of missing Your instruction...
a calling...a chance to do Your will.
Fear came. I was afraid to look for You.
What if You asked me to do something I didn't want to?
I ran from the voice I thought was Yours for so long.
Trust You? Place my life in Your hands?
"Only if you do this or that," the voice taunted at me.
I thought You wanted more of me than I was capable of giving.

Oh, Lord, comfort my soul when I believe these lies
that tell me You are just one more anxious thought away
from turning Your back.
Remind me of Your love.
Remind me of Your abundant grace.

The Lord will fulfill his purpose for me;
your steadfast love, O Lord, endures
forever. Do not forsake the work of your
hands.

Psalm 138:8 (ESV)

PRESENCE

What defines presence?
Specifically, God's presence.
I am learning that when we find
ourselves in a season where
He feels most far away, that's when we can
bet that He's doing a big work in us.

Sometimes He removes the feeling of His presence
so that we recognize our utter need for Him.
The best part about this work He is doing in our pain?
He never actually leaves us.
He's right at our bedside the whole time,
hand in ours as we wet our pillows with sobs so deep,
we think we'll never stop.

93

"One bold message in the Book of Job is that you can say anything to God. Throw at him your grief, your anger, your doubt, your bitterness, your betrayal, your disappointment—he can absorb them all. As often as not, spiritual giants of the Bible are shown contending with God. They prefer to go away limping, like Jacob, rather than to shut God out. In this respect, the Bible prefigures a tenet of modern psychology: you can't really deny your feelings or make them disappear, so you might as well express them. God can deal with every human response except one. He cannot abide the response I fall back on instinctively: an attempt to ignore him or treat him as though he does not exist. That response never once occurred to Job."

Philip Yancey

IN HIS HAND

You say You'll never let me out of Your hand.
But am I in it? How do I know? I've always
been on the outside of everything,
never fitting molds that seemed to be
created for everyone else but me.

I think about myself as a little girl.
I believed in You then.
I trusted that You were my helper.
It was simple and wholehearted.
You were my best friend.

When I work my way through the muck and
deafening noise of my anxious thoughts,
I hear You whisper, "You are mine"
I relax a little. Some days I believe it.
Other days I'm tempted to believe the lie
that I'm just holding on to hope.

But it's just that. A lie.
Your truth is true whether I believe it or not.
Make my heart believe.
When I am tossed about by waves of doubt,
calm the storm of my soul.

"God has not been trying an experiment on my faith or love in order to find out their quality. He knew it already. It was I who didn't. In this trial He makes us occupy the dock, the witness box, and the bench all at once. He always knew that my temple was a house of cards. His only way of making me realize the fact was to knock it down."

C.S. Lewis

DARKEST DARKNESS

I can't see out of the pain that I'm in.
Why is my brain working this way?
What they don't tell you about anxiety and depression is how
emotionally *and* physically painful it is.
Life has a dark shadow, consuming every ounce of hope.
It drains me of all my energy. I'm convinced I can't leave my home. I
can't eat. I can't even leave my bed today.
The darkness is so very dark.
Does my husband wish he made a different choice?
What will he do with me if I can't get out of this pit?
I am such a burden.

Lord, I look at my life and can't see any light.
I look to your Word, because my soul needs truth amidst the lies
coursing through every inch of me. You remind me that the darkness
will not overwhelm me.
Even the darkness is not dark to You.
Let me feel this truth.

O LORD, you have searched
me and known me!
You know when I sit down and
when I rise up;
you discern my thoughts from afar.
You search out my path
and my lying down
and are acquainted with all my ways.
Even before a word is on my tongue,
behold, O LORD, you know it altogether.
You hem me in, behind and before,
and lay your hand upon me.
Such knowledge is too wonderful for me;
it is high; I cannot attain it.

Where shall I go from your Spirit?
Or where shall I flee from your presence?
If I ascend to heaven, you are there!
If I make my bed in Sheol, you are there!
If I take the wings of the morning
and dwell in the uttermost parts of the sea,
even there your hand shall lead me,
and your right hand shall hold me.
If I say, **"Surely the darkness shall cover
me, and the light about me be night,"
even the darkness is not dark to you;
the night is bright as the day,
for darkness is as light with you.**

For you formed my inward parts;
you knitted me together in
my mother's womb.
I praise you, for I am fearfully and
wonderfully made.

Wonderful are your works;
my soul knows it very well.
My frame was not hidden from you,
when I was being made in secret,
intricately woven in the depths of the earth.
Your eyes saw my unformed substance;
in your book were written,
every one of them,
the days that were formed for me,
when as yet there was none of them.

How precious to me
are your thoughts, O God!
How vast is the sum of them!
If I would count them, they are
more than the sand.
I awake, and I am still with you.
Oh that you would slay
the wicked, O God!
O men of blood, depart from me!
They speak against you with
malicious intent;
your enemies take your name in vain.
Do I not hate those
who hate you, O LORD?
And do I not loathe those who rise
up against you?
I hate them with complete hatred;
I count them my enemies.
Search me, O God, and know my heart!
Try me and know my thoughts!
And see if there be any grievous way in me,
and lead me in the way everlasting!

Psalm 139 (ESV)

BROKEN PARADISE

Today I see glimpses of
what it could be.
Earth, I mean.

This broken paradise we live in.
I enter nature, and it's easy to see.
Mountains, rivers, oceans, forests...

Outside our small apartment,
there is a pond and some trees.
It's beautiful today.
It's 68 outside and sunny.
My perfect day.
I imagine for a moment

what it would be
to swim in the water
without the possibility
of serpents, poisonous algae
and bugs.

I imagine trees without ticks.
Oceans without stingrays.
Mountains without deathly drops
and dangerous creatures.

I imagine the sun without the sting of a
burn, and I'm reminded
that even nature has been

touched by the curse.
I'm thankful, though,
that God lets us see
what could be,
what will be.

For in trying times, we are
reminded of the hope
Jesus came to give us.
The hope that anchors the soul.

The curse is for a moment,
but His victory over it
allows us to endure.

MEANING TO THE MUNDANE

There's this period after conquering a hard season with the
Lord...
this wonderful,
peaceful,
joyous time.

Jesus is close by, and you can't help but weep daily with
gratitude at all He has taught you and brought you through.
This short season is what I like to call
the post-struggle-bus high.
Similar to, but not to be confused with, the
High-School-Church-Camp-Jesus High.

This blip of bliss is such a gift.
For me, it feels like I'm walking in the
Garden with my God.
I have a little more insight on His purpose
and His strength to carry me...
Fully felt.
Fully relied upon.
Fully known.

Like the familiar highs of the past, it doesn't last.
It feels like a cruel joke when this is snatched away and replaced.
Not by another trial or suffering, no,
but just simply with the *mundane*.
The stresses and annoyances of an every-day life
that we allow to lull us into
a sleepwalking state, drifting slowly away from
God with every swipe of our finger on our little screens.
Until another trial comes, and we don't even know
what has happened to us.

What of our relationship with God, then?
When the next affliction comes around,
will we be close by His side,
or will we look up to find ourselves
farther away from Him than we were before?

We must persevere.
Persevere through the days filled with nothingness
and the temptation to drift away.
Persevere so we stay close to
the One who gives meaning to the mundane.

Humble yourselves, therefore, under the mighty hand of God so that at the proper time he may exalt you, casting all your anxieties on him, because he cares for you. Be sober-minded; be watchful. Your adversary the devil prowls around like a roaring lion, seeking someone to devour. Resist him, firm in your faith, knowing that the **same kinds of suffering** are being experienced by your brotherhood throughout the world. And **after you have suffered a little while, the God of all grace, who has called you to his eternal glory in Christ, will himself restore, confirm, strengthen, and establish you.** To him be the dominion forever and ever. Amen.

1 Peter 5:6-11 (ESV)

REDEMPTION STORY

I feel the wild joy again.
I feel that You are good and kind.
I feel that You are trustworthy.
Oh, what a blessing it is when my feelings match up with the truth I know.
When I don't have to remind myself of it each day just to get through.
I feel as though I'm in a meadow, sun shining brightly on my face
and seeping into every inch of me.
Oh Lord, let me never forget what it feels like to be in the wilderness.
For in it, You create in me a new strength.
A new hope.
A new comfort.
A new redemption story.

"Poor human nature cannot bear such strains as heavenly triumphs bring to it; there must come a reaction. Excess of joy or excitement must be paid for by subsequent depressions. While the trial lasts, the strength is equal to the emergency; but when it is over, natural weakness claims the right to show itself."

Charles Spurgeon

GRATITUDE

Gratitude is like a lifeboat to my soul when it is in the pit. I begin listing everything I can, forcing all other thoughts out of my head, telling them that I'll get back to them another time.

The weather today.
My cozy bed.
Mac and cheese.
Sunsets.
A roof over my head.
The ability to buy groceries without stress.
A dishwasher.
Laundry machines in my home.
My husband.
My family.
My community.
My life.
My depression and anxiety...

Yes, even those. Why? For because of them, I am able to know deeply how dark the soul can feel. And because of that, my empathy knows no bounds. And finally, because of that, I am able to write this in a book for others to read and hopefully find comfort in the fact that they are not alone in this journey.

So friend, thank God today for your trials. Pray He will show you how to use them. For He does not give us sufferings in this life that are irredeemable. Your pain will one day be someone else's comfort. Your story, another's hope.

A PERSONAL NOTE
TO THE READER

Dear reader and fellow wanderer,

If you empathize with my writings in this book, specifically the ones that hint at doubt, my greatest encouragement to you would be to reach out to someone trustworthy to walk with you in your doubt, pain and questioning. Deconstruction is a hot topic during the time I am first releasing this book, and I pray that instead of letting your questions and feelings take you wherever they please, that you would resolve to trust Jesus now. Trust Him with every doubt. Pray that He would put you on a path of learning and growing in your faith in this season. This faith we wrestle with holds up to scrutiny. It is not a blind faith.

My prayer for everyone who reads this book is that you will not be scared of your questions, but will seek wise counsel and as a result, become comfortable in God's beautiful mysteries. I certainly do not have all the answers, but as someone who has battled an anxiety disorder, panic attacks, intrusive thought and depression - all in the midst of doubting my faith - take it from me, it is worth staying. Your hardest questions are worth exploring, but lay them at the feet of Jesus at the end of each day. Persevere, fellow saint. I will say it again: Persevere. You are not alone.

Love,

Shelby

NOTES

Philip Yancey quotations are taken from his various books and writings including: *Reaching for the Invisible God: What Can We Expect to Find?; Where Is God When It Hurts?; Disappointment with God: Three Questions No One Asks Aloud.*

Elisabeth Elliot quotation is from her book, *Suffering Is Never for Nothing.*

C.S. Lewis quotations are taken from his various books and writings including: *A Grief Observed; The Problem of Pain.*

Charles Spurgeon quotation is from "Lectures to My Students."

ACKNOWLEDGMENTS

Thank you to my grandparents, Paul and Billie, for creating a legacy of love and ministry for our family. The opportunity you have given me to publish this book is invaluable. I am so grateful for your love and support.

Mom and Dad, thank you for introducing me to Jesus. Thank you for praying for me from the moment you knew I was conceived and for always encouraging me in all my endeavors. You have always been my biggest fans. I know not everyone has parents who support the big dreams their kids have. You have never blinked at any of mine. Thank you from the bottom of my heart.

My husband, Cody. Your support is why I am still breathing, and why this book is here. You truly are my greatest treasure apart from Christ.

Our small group leaders, Mitch and Pam. You are an answered prayer for Cody and Me. Meeting you both, knowing you and learning from you has been a lifeboat for us and grown us spiritually in ways we will forever be grateful for. Your faith is actionable and is evident in the way you love and lead our little community so well. Mitch, you have walked with me carefully and intentionally through every question and doubt. Thank you for knowing the Word of God and loving Jesus. Thank you for never making me feel stupid for the questions I present you with. Without your counsel, I would still be drowning. I most definitely would not have created this book. I pray that every doubter would seek and find someone like you to walk with them in their questioning.

My personal counselor, Whitney. You deserve a lot of praise for walking with me in the midst of most of the junk I have written about in this book, plus so much more. Your merciful way of guiding me bravely through so many of my fears, mental health struggles and doubts has been the greatest gift. Thank you for loving Jesus and pointing me to Him in every battle I face.

To all the friends whose conversations have inspired some of the reflections on these pages, thank you for letting me wrestle with and do life with you.

This book was birthed out of the hardest seasons of my life. I wouldn't be where I am in my faith life or have the perspective on suffering that I do without the people mentioned above. Words are utterly inadequate to express the gratitude I feel toward each of you.

.

PAUL E. TSIKA MINISTRIES INC.

46 E Kitty Hawk St
Richmond, TX 77406

www.plowon.org

(833)999-9661